50 Date Night Dessert Recipes for Home

By: Kelly Johnson

Table of Contents

- Molten Chocolate Lava Cakes
- Tiramisu
- Raspberry White Chocolate Mousse
- Chocolate Covered Strawberries
- Creme Brulee
- Panna Cotta with Berry Compote
- Apple Pie with Vanilla Ice Cream
- Flourless Chocolate Cake
- Lemon Sorbet
- Red Velvet Cupcakes
- Chocolate Fondue with Dipping Goodies
- Mango Coconut Rice Pudding
- Blueberry Cheesecake Bars
- Nutella Stuffed Crepes
- Espresso Chocolate Mousse
- Peanut Butter Chocolate Chip Cookies
- Poached Pears in Red Wine
- Strawberry Shortcake
- Chocolate Turtles
- Dark Chocolate Avocado Mousse
- Salted Caramel Brownies
- Key Lime Pie
- Mini Cheesecakes with Fruit Topping
- Banana Foster
- Black Forest Cake
- Cherry Almond Clafoutis
- Almond Joy Truffles
- Lemon Bars
- Chocolate Raspberry Tart
- Cinnamon Sugar Churros
- Vanilla Bean Pudding
- Coconut Macaroons
- Pistachio Ice Cream
- Mocha Pots de Creme
- Chocolate Dipped Pretzels

- Bourbon Pecan Pie
- Pineapple Upside-Down Cake
- Mango Sorbet
- Oreo Cheesecake Bites
- Maple Pecan Blondies
- Peach Cobbler
- Cannoli
- Dark Chocolate and Sea Salt Caramel Tart
- Strawberry Tiramisu
- Raspberry Chocolate Tart
- Coffee and Walnut Cake
- Orange Chocolate Mousse
- S'mores Dip
- Lemon Poppy Seed Cake
- Gingerbread Cookies

Molten Chocolate Lava Cakes

Ingredients:

- 1/2 cup unsalted butter
- 4 ounces high-quality dark chocolate (70% cocoa), chopped
- 2 large eggs
- 2 egg yolks
- 1/4 cup granulated sugar
- 1 teaspoon vanilla extract
- 2 tablespoons all-purpose flour
- Pinch of salt
- Cocoa powder and powdered sugar for dusting
- Vanilla ice cream or whipped cream for serving (optional)

Instructions:

Preheat Oven:
- Preheat your oven to 425°F (220°C). Grease and flour 4 ramekins or custard cups.

Melt Chocolate and Butter:
- In a heatproof bowl set over a pot of simmering water (double boiler), melt the butter and chopped dark chocolate, stirring until smooth. Remove from heat and let it cool slightly.

Prepare Batter:
- In a separate bowl, whisk together the eggs, egg yolks, granulated sugar, and vanilla extract until well combined.

Combine Chocolate and Egg Mixtures:
- Slowly pour the melted chocolate mixture into the egg mixture, whisking continuously to avoid scrambling the eggs.

Add Flour and Salt:
- Sift in the all-purpose flour and add a pinch of salt. Gently fold the dry ingredients into the chocolate mixture until just combined.

Fill Ramekins:
- Divide the batter evenly among the prepared ramekins.

Bake:
- Place the ramekins on a baking sheet and bake in the preheated oven for 12-14 minutes, or until the edges are set but the center is still soft.

Cool Slightly:
- Allow the lava cakes to cool for a minute or two. They should be firm enough to hold their shape but still have a molten center.

Serve:
- Run a knife around the edges of the ramekins to loosen the cakes. Invert each cake onto a plate, tapping the bottom gently.

Dust and Garnish:
- Dust the tops with cocoa powder and powdered sugar. You can also add a scoop of vanilla ice cream or a dollop of whipped cream if desired.

Serve Immediately:
- Serve the Molten Chocolate Lava Cakes immediately while they are warm and gooey.

Enjoy:
- Indulge in the decadent pleasure of breaking into the molten center of these delightful chocolate treats.

Tiramisu

Ingredients:

- 4 large egg yolks
- 3/4 cup granulated sugar
- 1 cup mascarpone cheese, softened
- 1 1/2 cups heavy cream
- 1 cup strong brewed coffee or espresso, cooled
- 1/4 cup coffee liqueur (like Kahlúa), optional
- 1 teaspoon vanilla extract
- 24-30 ladyfinger cookies
- Unsweetened cocoa powder, for dusting
- Chocolate shavings or grated chocolate, for garnish

Instructions:

Brew Coffee:
- Brew a strong cup of coffee or espresso. Allow it to cool to room temperature.

Prepare Mascarpone Mixture:
- In a mixing bowl, whisk together the egg yolks and granulated sugar until the mixture becomes pale and slightly thickened.
- Add the softened mascarpone cheese to the egg yolk mixture and beat until smooth and well combined.

Whip Heavy Cream:
- In a separate bowl, whip the heavy cream until stiff peaks form.

Combine Mascarpone and Whipped Cream:
- Gently fold the whipped cream into the mascarpone mixture until you have a smooth and creamy consistency.

Add Coffee Flavor:
- If using, stir in the coffee liqueur and vanilla extract into the mascarpone mixture.

Assemble Tiramisu:
- Dip each ladyfinger into the brewed coffee briefly, ensuring they are soaked but not overly soggy. Arrange a layer of dipped ladyfingers in the bottom of a serving dish or individual glasses.
- Spread half of the mascarpone mixture over the layer of ladyfingers.

- Repeat with another layer of dipped ladyfingers and the remaining mascarpone mixture.

Chill:
- Cover the tiramisu with plastic wrap and refrigerate for at least 4 hours, preferably overnight, to allow the flavors to meld and the dessert to set.

Dust with Cocoa Powder:
- Before serving, dust the top of the tiramisu with unsweetened cocoa powder using a fine-mesh sieve.

Garnish:
- Optionally, garnish with chocolate shavings or grated chocolate.

Serve:
- Serve chilled and enjoy this classic Tiramisu as a delightful and elegant dessert.

Raspberry White Chocolate Mousse

Ingredients:

- 1 cup fresh raspberries
- 1/4 cup granulated sugar
- 1 tablespoon lemon juice
- 2 teaspoons gelatin powder
- 2 tablespoons water
- 8 ounces white chocolate, chopped
- 2 cups heavy cream
- 1 teaspoon vanilla extract
- Fresh raspberries for garnish
- White chocolate shavings for garnish

Instructions:

Prepare Raspberry Puree:
- In a blender or food processor, puree the fresh raspberries with granulated sugar and lemon juice until smooth. Strain the mixture through a fine-mesh sieve to remove seeds. Set aside.

Bloom Gelatin:
- In a small bowl, mix gelatin powder with water and let it sit for 5 minutes to bloom.

Melt White Chocolate:
- In a heatproof bowl, melt the chopped white chocolate over a double boiler or in the microwave in short bursts, stirring until smooth. Allow it to cool slightly.

Combine Raspberry Puree and Gelatin:
- Warm the raspberry puree slightly and stir in the bloomed gelatin. Mix until the gelatin is completely dissolved in the puree.

Add Raspberry Mixture to White Chocolate:
- Gradually whisk the raspberry and gelatin mixture into the melted white chocolate until well combined.

Whip Heavy Cream:
- In a separate bowl, whip the heavy cream until stiff peaks form.

Fold in Whipped Cream:

- Gently fold the whipped cream into the raspberry and white chocolate mixture until smooth and evenly combined.

Chill:
- Divide the mousse into serving glasses or bowls. Refrigerate for at least 4 hours, allowing the mousse to set.

Garnish:
- Before serving, garnish with fresh raspberries and white chocolate shavings.

Serve:
- Serve chilled and savor the delightful combination of raspberry and white chocolate in this light and airy mousse.

Chocolate Covered Strawberries

Ingredients:

- Fresh strawberries, washed and dried
- 8 ounces high-quality dark or milk chocolate, chopped
- White chocolate (optional, for drizzling)
- Toppings (chopped nuts, shredded coconut, sprinkles, etc., optional)

Instructions:

Prepare Strawberries:
- Make sure the strawberries are completely dry. Water can cause the chocolate to seize.

Melt Dark or Milk Chocolate:
- In a heatproof bowl set over a pot of simmering water (double boiler) or in the microwave in short bursts, melt the dark or milk chocolate until smooth.

Dip Strawberries:
- Hold each strawberry by the stem and dip it into the melted chocolate, covering about two-thirds of the berry. Allow excess chocolate to drip off.

Place on Parchment Paper:
- Place the chocolate-covered strawberries on a parchment paper-lined tray. This prevents them from sticking and makes for easy cleanup.

Cool and Set:
- Allow the chocolate-covered strawberries to cool and set at room temperature. You can speed up the process by placing them in the refrigerator for about 15-20 minutes.

Optional: Melt White Chocolate:
- If desired, melt white chocolate using the same method as before.

Drizzle with White Chocolate (Optional):
- Once the dark or milk chocolate has set, drizzle the strawberries with melted white chocolate for a decorative touch.

Add Toppings (Optional):
- While the white chocolate is still wet, sprinkle or roll the strawberries in toppings like chopped nuts, shredded coconut, or sprinkles.

Final Set:

- Allow the chocolate-covered strawberries to set completely. This can be done in the refrigerator for an additional 15-20 minutes.

Serve:
- Arrange the chocolate-covered strawberries on a serving plate or present them in a decorative box for a romantic touch.

Enjoy:
- Indulge in these delicious and elegant Chocolate Covered Strawberries for a sweet and simple treat!

Creme Brulee

Ingredients:

- 2 cups heavy cream
- 1 vanilla bean, split and seeds scraped (or 1 teaspoon vanilla extract)
- 5 large egg yolks
- 1/2 cup granulated sugar, plus extra for caramelizing
- Pinch of salt

Instructions:

Preheat Oven:
- Preheat your oven to 325°F (163°C). Place oven racks in the middle position.

Prepare Ramekins:
- Arrange six 6-ounce ramekins in a baking dish or on a baking sheet.

Heat Cream and Vanilla:
- In a saucepan, heat the heavy cream and vanilla seeds (or vanilla extract) over medium heat until it just starts to simmer. Remove from heat and let it steep for about 15 minutes.

Whisk Egg Yolks and Sugar:
- In a mixing bowl, whisk together the egg yolks, granulated sugar, and a pinch of salt until the mixture is pale and slightly thickened.

Combine Cream and Eggs:
- Gradually pour the warm cream mixture into the egg yolk mixture, stirring constantly to avoid curdling. Strain the mixture through a fine-mesh sieve into a large bowl.

Fill Ramekins:
- Divide the custard mixture evenly among the ramekins.

Bake in Water Bath:
- Place the baking dish with the ramekins in the preheated oven. Pour hot water into the baking dish to come halfway up the sides of the ramekins. This creates a water bath that ensures gentle and even cooking.

Bake Until Set:
- Bake for 30-40 minutes or until the edges are set, but the center still jiggles slightly when tapped.

Chill:

- Remove the ramekins from the water bath and let them cool to room temperature. Then, refrigerate for at least 4 hours, preferably overnight.

Caramelize Sugar:
- Just before serving, sprinkle a thin, even layer of granulated sugar over each custard. Use a kitchen torch to caramelize the sugar until it forms a golden-brown crust.

Serve:
- Allow the Crème Brûlée to sit for a moment to let the sugar harden. Serve immediately.

Enjoy:
- Break through the crunchy caramelized layer to indulge in the creamy goodness of this classic Crème Brûlée.

Panna Cotta with Berry Compote

Ingredients:

For Panna Cotta:

- 2 cups heavy cream
- 1/2 cup whole milk
- 1/2 cup granulated sugar
- 2 teaspoons vanilla extract
- 2 1/4 teaspoons (1 packet) gelatin powder
- 3 tablespoons cold water

For Berry Compote:

- 1 cup mixed berries (strawberries, blueberries, raspberries)
- 1/4 cup granulated sugar
- 1 tablespoon lemon juice
- Zest of one lemon

Instructions:

Panna Cotta:

Prepare Gelatin:
- In a small bowl, sprinkle gelatin over cold water. Let it sit for 5-10 minutes to bloom.

Warm Cream and Sugar:
- In a saucepan, heat the heavy cream, whole milk, and granulated sugar over medium heat. Stir until the sugar is dissolved and the mixture is warmed.

Add Gelatin:
- Add the bloomed gelatin to the warm cream mixture. Stir until the gelatin is completely dissolved.

Flavor with Vanilla:
- Remove the saucepan from heat and stir in the vanilla extract.

Pour into Molds:

- Divide the mixture into serving glasses or molds. Allow them to cool to room temperature before placing them in the refrigerator to set. Let them chill for at least 4 hours or overnight.

Berry Compote:

Prepare Berries:
- In a saucepan, combine mixed berries, granulated sugar, lemon juice, and lemon zest.

Cook Berry Mixture:
- Cook over medium heat, stirring occasionally, until the berries break down and release their juices. Simmer for about 10-15 minutes until the mixture thickens slightly.

Cool:
- Allow the berry compote to cool to room temperature.

Assemble:

Serve:
- Once the Panna Cotta has set, spoon a generous amount of berry compote over the top.

Garnish (Optional):
- Garnish with fresh berries or a mint sprig for an extra touch.

Enjoy:
- Indulge in the creamy delight of Panna Cotta with the vibrant burst of flavor from the mixed berry compote.

Apple Pie with Vanilla Ice Cream

Ingredients:

For the Pie Filling:

- 6 cups peeled, cored, and sliced apples (such as Granny Smith or a mix of varieties)
- 3/4 cup granulated sugar
- 1 tablespoon lemon juice
- 2 tablespoons all-purpose flour
- 1 teaspoon ground cinnamon
- 1/4 teaspoon ground nutmeg
- 1/4 teaspoon salt

For the Pie Crust:

- 2 1/2 cups all-purpose flour
- 1 cup unsalted butter, cold and cubed
- 1 teaspoon salt
- 1 tablespoon granulated sugar
- 6-8 tablespoons ice water

For Serving:

- Vanilla ice cream

Instructions:

Pie Filling:

>Preheat Oven:
>- Preheat your oven to 375°F (190°C).
>
>Prepare Apples:
>- In a large bowl, toss the sliced apples with lemon juice to prevent browning.
>
>Combine Dry Ingredients:

- In a separate bowl, mix together sugar, flour, cinnamon, nutmeg, and salt.

Coat Apples:
- Sprinkle the dry ingredient mixture over the apples and toss until the apples are evenly coated.

Pie Crust:

Prepare Pie Crust:
- In a food processor, combine flour, salt, and sugar. Add the cold, cubed butter and pulse until the mixture resembles coarse crumbs.

Add Ice Water:
- With the processor running, add ice water one tablespoon at a time until the dough starts to come together.

Form Dough:
- Turn the dough out onto a floured surface and knead it gently until it forms a ball. Divide the dough in half.

Roll Out Crust:
- Roll out one half of the dough to fit a 9-inch pie dish. Place the rolled-out crust into the pie dish.

Add Apple Filling:
- Spoon the prepared apple filling into the crust.

Top with Second Crust:
- Roll out the second half of the dough and place it over the apple filling. Trim and crimp the edges to seal the pie.

Ventilation:
- Cut slits in the top crust to allow steam to escape during baking.

Bake:
- Bake in the preheated oven for about 45-50 minutes or until the crust is golden brown and the filling is bubbly.

Cool:
- Allow the pie to cool for at least 2 hours before serving.

Serve:

Slice and Serve:
- Slice the apple pie into wedges and serve with a scoop of vanilla ice cream on top.

Enjoy:

- Enjoy the comforting combination of warm apple pie and cold vanilla ice cream for a delightful treat!

Flourless Chocolate Cake

Ingredients:

- 1 cup (2 sticks) unsalted butter
- 1 1/2 cups semi-sweet or bittersweet chocolate chips or coarsely chopped chocolate
- 1 cup granulated sugar
- 1/2 cup unsweetened cocoa powder
- 1/4 teaspoon salt
- 1 teaspoon instant coffee or espresso powder (optional)
- 1 teaspoon vanilla extract
- 5 large eggs, room temperature

Instructions:

Preheat Oven:
- Preheat your oven to 375°F (190°C). Grease a 9-inch round cake pan and line the bottom with parchment paper.

Melt Chocolate and Butter:
- In a heatproof bowl set over a pot of simmering water (double boiler) or in the microwave, melt together the butter and chocolate until smooth. Stir in the instant coffee or espresso powder if using.

Add Sugar and Cocoa:
- Remove the melted chocolate mixture from heat and whisk in the granulated sugar, cocoa powder, and salt until well combined.

Incorporate Eggs:
- Whisk in the vanilla extract, and then add the eggs one at a time, whisking well after each addition.

Batter Consistency:
- The batter will be thick and glossy.

Bake:
- Pour the batter into the prepared cake pan and smooth the top.

Bake in Water Bath (Optional):
- You can choose to bake the cake in a water bath for a more delicate texture. Place the cake pan in a larger roasting pan, and fill the roasting pan with hot water until it reaches about halfway up the sides of the cake pan.

Bake Time:
- Bake in the preheated oven for 25-30 minutes, or until a toothpick inserted into the center comes out with moist crumbs (not wet batter).

Cool:
- Allow the cake to cool in the pan for about 10 minutes, then transfer it to a wire rack to cool completely.

Chill (Optional):
- For an even denser texture, you can refrigerate the cake for a few hours or overnight.

Serve:
- Slice and serve the flourless chocolate cake on its own or with a dusting of powdered sugar, a dollop of whipped cream, or a scoop of vanilla ice cream.

Enjoy:
- Indulge in the rich and decadent flavor of this flourless chocolate cake!

Lemon Sorbet

Ingredients:

- 1 cup granulated sugar
- 1 cup water
- 1 cup fresh lemon juice (about 4-6 lemons)
- 1 tablespoon lemon zest (from about 2 lemons)

Instructions:

Simple Syrup:
- In a saucepan, combine the sugar and water. Heat over medium heat, stirring occasionally, until the sugar completely dissolves. Allow the mixture to cool to room temperature to create a simple syrup.

Extract Lemon Juice:
- While the simple syrup is cooling, extract fresh lemon juice from the lemons. You can use a citrus juicer or squeeze them by hand. Strain the juice to remove any seeds and pulp.

Combine Lemon Juice and Zest:
- In a bowl, combine the fresh lemon juice and lemon zest. Stir to incorporate the flavors.

Create Sorbet Base:
- Once the simple syrup has cooled, add it to the lemon juice mixture. Stir well to combine, creating the sorbet base.

Chill Mixture:
- Cover the bowl and refrigerate the mixture for at least 2 hours to chill thoroughly.

Churn in Ice Cream Maker:
- Pour the chilled lemon sorbet base into an ice cream maker and churn according to the manufacturer's instructions. This typically takes about 20-30 minutes.

Transfer to Freezer-Safe Container:
- Transfer the churned sorbet into a freezer-safe container. Smooth the top with a spatula.

Freeze:
- Freeze the sorbet for at least 4 hours or until firm.

Serve:

- Prior to serving, let the lemon sorbet sit at room temperature for a few minutes to soften slightly. Scoop into bowls or cones.

Garnish (Optional):
- Garnish with a twist of lemon zest or a mint sprig if desired.

Enjoy:
- Refresh yourself with the vibrant and citrusy taste of homemade lemon sorbet. It's a delightful and cooling treat, especially on warm days!

Red Velvet Cupcakes

Ingredients:

For the Cupcakes:

- 1 1/2 cups all-purpose flour
- 1 cup granulated sugar
- 1/2 teaspoon baking powder
- 1/2 teaspoon baking soda
- 1/4 teaspoon salt
- 2 tablespoons cocoa powder
- 3/4 cup vegetable oil
- 1 cup buttermilk, room temperature
- 2 large eggs, room temperature
- 2 tablespoons red food coloring
- 1 teaspoon vanilla extract
- 1 teaspoon white vinegar

For the Cream Cheese Frosting:

- 8 ounces cream cheese, softened
- 1/2 cup unsalted butter, softened
- 4 cups powdered sugar
- 1 teaspoon vanilla extract

Instructions:

Red Velvet Cupcakes:

Preheat Oven:
- Preheat your oven to 350°F (180°C). Line a cupcake tin with paper liners.

Combine Dry Ingredients:
- In a bowl, sift together flour, sugar, baking powder, baking soda, salt, and cocoa powder.

Mix Wet Ingredients:
- In another bowl, whisk together oil, buttermilk, eggs, red food coloring, vanilla extract, and white vinegar.

Combine Wet and Dry Mixtures:

- Gradually add the wet ingredients to the dry ingredients, mixing until just combined. Be careful not to overmix.

Fill Cupcake Liners:
- Divide the batter evenly among the cupcake liners, filling each about 2/3 full.

Bake:
- Bake in the preheated oven for 18-20 minutes or until a toothpick inserted into the center of a cupcake comes out clean.

Cool:
- Allow the cupcakes to cool in the tin for a few minutes, then transfer them to a wire rack to cool completely.

Cream Cheese Frosting:

Beat Cream Cheese and Butter:
- In a mixing bowl, beat together softened cream cheese and butter until smooth and creamy.

Add Powdered Sugar:
- Gradually add powdered sugar, one cup at a time, beating well after each addition until the frosting is smooth.

Incorporate Vanilla Extract:
- Mix in the vanilla extract until well combined.

Frost Cupcakes:
- Once the cupcakes are completely cooled, frost them with the cream cheese frosting. You can use a piping bag or simply spread the frosting with a spatula.

Optional: Decorate:
- Optionally, decorate the cupcakes with red velvet crumbs, sprinkles, or any desired toppings.

Serve:
- Arrange the red velvet cupcakes on a serving platter and enjoy these classic treats!

Note: Adjust the amount of red food coloring according to your preference for a deeper or lighter red hue.

Chocolate Fondue with Dipping Goodies

Ingredients:

For the Chocolate Fondue:

- 8 ounces dark chocolate, finely chopped
- 1 cup heavy cream
- 1 teaspoon vanilla extract
- 2 tablespoons unsalted butter

For Dipping Goodies:

- Strawberries, washed and hulled
- Bananas, sliced
- Pineapple chunks
- Pretzel sticks
- Marshmallows
- Cubes of pound cake or angel food cake
- Cookies (such as biscotti or shortbread)

Instructions:

Chocolate Fondue:

    Prepare Chocolate:
- Place the finely chopped dark chocolate in a heatproof bowl.

    Heat Cream:
- In a saucepan, heat the heavy cream over medium heat until it just starts to simmer. Do not let it boil.

    Pour over Chocolate:
- Pour the hot cream over the chopped chocolate. Let it sit for a minute to melt the chocolate.

    Stir until Smooth:
- Stir the chocolate and cream mixture until smooth and well combined.

    Add Butter and Vanilla:

- Add the unsalted butter and vanilla extract to the chocolate mixture. Stir until the butter is melted and the fondue is smooth.

Transfer to Fondue Pot:
- Transfer the chocolate fondue to a fondue pot or a heatproof serving bowl. Keep warm over a low flame.

Dipping Goodies:

Prepare Dipping Items:
- Wash and prepare the fruits, slice the bananas, cut the pound cake into cubes, and arrange the marshmallows and other goodies on a serving platter.

Serve:
- Place the platter of dipping goodies next to the chocolate fondue pot.

Dip and Enjoy:
- Use fondue forks or skewers to dip the various goodies into the warm chocolate fondue. Swirl them around to coat them in the delicious chocolate.

Variations:
- Get creative with additional dipping options like chopped nuts, dried fruits, or even potato chips for a sweet and salty combination.

Reheat if Necessary:
- If the chocolate fondue starts to thicken, you can gently reheat it over low heat or in the microwave, stirring until smooth.

Enjoy:
- Enjoy the delightful experience of chocolate fondue with an assortment of delicious dipping goodies. Perfect for parties or a romantic dessert!

Mango Coconut Rice Pudding

Ingredients:

- 1 cup Arborio rice
- 1 can (14 ounces) coconut milk
- 2 cups whole milk
- 1/2 cup granulated sugar
- 1 teaspoon vanilla extract
- 1/4 teaspoon salt
- 1 large ripe mango, peeled, pitted, and diced
- Toasted coconut flakes for garnish (optional)

Instructions:

Rinse Rice:
- Rinse the Arborio rice under cold water until the water runs clear. This helps remove excess starch.

Cook Rice:
- In a medium saucepan, combine the rinsed rice, coconut milk, whole milk, sugar, vanilla extract, and salt.

Bring to a Simmer:
- Bring the mixture to a simmer over medium heat, stirring frequently to prevent the rice from sticking to the bottom.

Simmer Until Tender:
- Reduce the heat to low and let the rice simmer gently for about 25-30 minutes or until the rice is tender and the mixture has thickened.

Add Mango:
- Once the rice is cooked, fold in the diced mango and continue to cook for an additional 5 minutes to allow the flavors to meld.

Adjust Sweetness:
- Taste the pudding and adjust the sweetness if needed by adding more sugar, if desired.

Serve:
- Remove the rice pudding from heat and let it cool slightly. Spoon it into serving bowls.

Chill (Optional):

- You can refrigerate the rice pudding for a few hours to serve it chilled, or serve it warm.

Garnish:
- Garnish with toasted coconut flakes for added flavor and texture.

Serve:
- Serve the Mango Coconut Rice Pudding as a delicious and tropical dessert.

Enjoy:
- Enjoy the creamy and flavorful combination of coconut, mango, and rice in this delightful rice pudding!

Blueberry Cheesecake Bars

Ingredients:

For the Crust:

- 1 1/2 cups graham cracker crumbs
- 1/2 cup unsalted butter, melted
- 1/4 cup granulated sugar

For the Cheesecake Layer:

- 16 ounces (2 packages) cream cheese, softened
- 1/2 cup granulated sugar
- 2 large eggs
- 1 teaspoon vanilla extract
- 1 tablespoon all-purpose flour

For the Blueberry Topping:

- 1 1/2 cups fresh or frozen blueberries
- 1/4 cup granulated sugar
- 1 tablespoon lemon juice
- 1 tablespoon cornstarch

Instructions:

Crust:

> Preheat Oven:
> - Preheat your oven to 350°F (175°C). Line a 9x9-inch baking pan with parchment paper, leaving an overhang for easy removal.
>
> Mix Crust Ingredients:
> - In a bowl, combine graham cracker crumbs, melted butter, and sugar. Mix until the crumbs are evenly coated.
>
> Press into Pan:

- Press the mixture into the bottom of the prepared pan to form an even crust.

Bake:
- Bake the crust in the preheated oven for 8-10 minutes or until set. Remove from the oven and let it cool while preparing the cheesecake layer.

Cheesecake Layer:

Beat Cream Cheese:
- In a mixing bowl, beat the softened cream cheese until smooth and creamy.

Add Sugar:
- Add the granulated sugar and continue to beat until well combined.

Incorporate Eggs:
- Add the eggs one at a time, beating well after each addition.

Add Vanilla and Flour:
- Mix in the vanilla extract and flour until the batter is smooth.

Spread Over Crust:
- Spread the cream cheese mixture evenly over the cooled crust.

Blueberry Topping:

Prepare Blueberries:
- In a saucepan, combine blueberries, sugar, lemon juice, and cornstarch.

Cook:
- Cook over medium heat, stirring constantly, until the mixture thickens and the blueberries burst. This usually takes about 5-7 minutes.

Cool Slightly:
- Let the blueberry topping cool slightly.

Spread Over Cheesecake Layer:
- Gently spread the blueberry topping over the cream cheese layer in the pan.

Chill:
- Place the pan in the refrigerator and chill for at least 4 hours or overnight to set.

Slice and Serve:
- Once fully chilled and set, use the parchment paper overhang to lift the bars from the pan. Cut into squares and serve.

Optional: Garnish:
- Garnish with additional fresh blueberries or a dusting of powdered sugar if desired.

Enjoy:
- Enjoy these delicious Blueberry Cheesecake Bars as a delightful treat!

Nutella Stuffed Crepes

Ingredients:

For the Crepes:

- 1 cup all-purpose flour
- 2 large eggs
- 1 cup milk
- 1/4 cup water
- 2 tablespoons melted butter
- 1 tablespoon granulated sugar
- 1/4 teaspoon salt

For the Filling:

- Nutella (as needed)
- Sliced strawberries, bananas, or other fruits (optional)
- Chopped nuts (optional)
- Powdered sugar for dusting

Instructions:

Crepes:

Prepare Batter:
- In a blender, combine flour, eggs, milk, water, melted butter, sugar, and salt. Blend until the batter is smooth. Let the batter rest for at least 30 minutes in the refrigerator.

Heat Skillet:
- Heat a non-stick skillet or crepe pan over medium heat. Lightly grease with butter or cooking spray.

Cook Crepes:
- Pour a small amount of batter (about 1/4 cup) into the center of the hot skillet. Quickly tilt the pan to spread the batter thinly and evenly.

Cook Until Set:

- Cook the crepe for about 1-2 minutes or until the edges start to lightly brown. Flip the crepe using a spatula and cook the other side for an additional 1-2 minutes.

Repeat:
- Repeat the process with the remaining batter, stacking the cooked crepes on a plate.

Assemble Nutella Stuffed Crepes:

Spread Nutella:
- Lay a crepe flat on a serving plate. Spread a generous amount of Nutella over one half of the crepe.

Add Fruits and Nuts (Optional):
- Add sliced strawberries, bananas, or other fruits of your choice over the Nutella. Sprinkle with chopped nuts if desired.

Fold and Serve:
- Fold the crepe in half to cover the Nutella and filling. Fold it in half again if you prefer a triangular shape.

Repeat:
- Repeat the process with the remaining crepes and fillings.

Dust with Powdered Sugar:
- Dust the Nutella stuffed crepes with powdered sugar just before serving.

Serve Warm:
- Serve the Nutella stuffed crepes warm and enjoy this delightful, indulgent treat!

Optional:

- You can also drizzle additional Nutella on top or add a scoop of vanilla ice cream for an extra decadent experience.

Espresso Chocolate Mousse

Ingredients:

- 6 ounces (170g) dark chocolate, chopped
- 3 tablespoons strong brewed espresso or instant coffee, cooled
- 3 large eggs, separated
- 1/4 cup granulated sugar
- 1 teaspoon vanilla extract
- 1 cup heavy cream
- Chocolate shavings or cocoa powder for garnish (optional)

Instructions:

Melt Chocolate:
- In a heatproof bowl set over simmering water (double boiler) or using a microwave, melt the chopped dark chocolate until smooth. Remove from heat and let it cool slightly.

Add Espresso:
- Stir in the brewed espresso or instant coffee into the melted chocolate. Mix until well combined. Let it cool to room temperature.

Separate Eggs:
- Separate the egg yolks from the whites. Place the egg yolks in one bowl and the egg whites in another.

Beat Egg Yolks:
- In the bowl with egg yolks, whisk them together with granulated sugar until the mixture becomes pale and slightly thickened.

Incorporate Chocolate Mixture:
- Pour the melted chocolate-espresso mixture into the egg yolk mixture, and stir until well combined. Add vanilla extract and mix.

Whip Egg Whites:
- In a clean, dry bowl, whip the egg whites using an electric mixer until stiff peaks form.

Fold in Egg Whites:
- Gently fold the whipped egg whites into the chocolate mixture until no white streaks remain. Be careful not to deflate the egg whites.

Whip Heavy Cream:
- In another bowl, whip the heavy cream until stiff peaks form.

Fold in Whipped Cream:
- Gently fold the whipped cream into the chocolate mixture until smooth and creamy.

Chill:
- Spoon the espresso chocolate mousse into serving glasses or bowls. Chill in the refrigerator for at least 2-3 hours or until set.

Garnish (Optional):
- Before serving, garnish with chocolate shavings or a dusting of cocoa powder if desired.

Serve:
- Serve the Espresso Chocolate Mousse chilled and enjoy the rich and indulgent flavors!

Note:

- For an extra kick, you can add a tablespoon of coffee liqueur to the chocolate mixture before folding in the whipped cream. Adjust the sweetness according to your preference.

Peanut Butter Chocolate Chip Cookies

Ingredients:

- 1/2 cup unsalted butter, softened
- 1/2 cup creamy peanut butter
- 1/2 cup granulated sugar
- 1/2 cup packed light brown sugar
- 1 large egg
- 1 teaspoon vanilla extract
- 1 1/4 cups all-purpose flour
- 1/2 teaspoon baking powder
- 1/2 teaspoon baking soda
- 1/4 teaspoon salt
- 1 cup chocolate chips

Instructions:

Preheat Oven:
- Preheat your oven to 350°F (175°C). Line baking sheets with parchment paper.

Cream Butter and Sugars:
- In a large mixing bowl, cream together the softened butter, peanut butter, granulated sugar, and brown sugar until light and fluffy.

Add Egg and Vanilla:
- Add the egg and vanilla extract to the butter-sugar mixture. Beat until well combined.

Combine Dry Ingredients:
- In a separate bowl, whisk together the flour, baking powder, baking soda, and salt.

Mix Wet and Dry Ingredients:
- Gradually add the dry ingredients to the wet ingredients, mixing until just combined.

Add Chocolate Chips:
- Fold in the chocolate chips until evenly distributed throughout the cookie dough.

Scoop Dough:

- Use a cookie scoop or spoon to drop rounded tablespoons of dough onto the prepared baking sheets, spacing them about 2 inches apart.

Flatten (Optional):
- You can gently flatten each cookie with a fork if you prefer a flatter shape.

Bake:
- Bake in the preheated oven for 10-12 minutes or until the edges are golden brown.

Cool on Pan:
- Allow the cookies to cool on the baking sheets for a few minutes before transferring them to a wire rack to cool completely.

Store:
- Once completely cooled, store the Peanut Butter Chocolate Chip Cookies in an airtight container.

Enjoy:
- Enjoy these delicious, classic cookies with the perfect combination of peanut butter and chocolate!

Note:

- Feel free to use crunchy peanut butter for added texture or mix in chopped nuts of your choice if desired.

Poached Pears in Red Wine

Ingredients:

- 4 firm but ripe pears (such as Bosc or Anjou), peeled and cored
- 1 bottle (750 ml) red wine (Merlot, Cabernet Sauvignon, or red blend)
- 1 cup granulated sugar
- 1 cinnamon stick
- 1 vanilla bean, split lengthwise (or 1 teaspoon vanilla extract)
- Zest of one orange
- Whipped cream or vanilla ice cream for serving (optional)
- Fresh mint leaves for garnish (optional)

Instructions:

Prepare Pears:
- Peel and core the pears, leaving them whole.

Poaching Liquid:
- In a large saucepan, combine the red wine, granulated sugar, cinnamon stick, vanilla bean (or vanilla extract), and orange zest.

Bring to a Simmer:
- Place the saucepan over medium heat and bring the liquid to a gentle simmer, stirring to dissolve the sugar.

Add Pears:
- Gently place the peeled and cored pears into the simmering liquid.

Poach:
- Allow the pears to poach in the red wine mixture for about 20-30 minutes or until they are tender but not mushy. You can occasionally baste the pears with the liquid.

Test for Doneness:
- To test for doneness, insert a knife into the pears; it should go in easily.

Remove Pears:
- Once the pears are poached, carefully remove them from the liquid and set them aside.

Reduce Poaching Liquid:
- Increase the heat and bring the poaching liquid to a boil. Let it simmer until it reduces and thickens into a syrup-like consistency.

Strain Liquid:

- If desired, strain the liquid to remove the cinnamon stick, vanilla bean, and orange zest.

Serve:
- Plate the poached pears and drizzle the reduced poaching liquid over them.

Optional: Whipped Cream or Ice Cream:
- Serve the poached pears with a dollop of whipped cream or a scoop of vanilla ice cream if desired.

Garnish (Optional):
- Garnish with fresh mint leaves for a burst of color.

Enjoy:
- Enjoy these elegant and flavorful Poached Pears in Red Wine as a delightful dessert!

Strawberry Shortcake

Ingredients:

For the Shortcakes:

- 2 cups all-purpose flour
- 1/4 cup granulated sugar
- 1 tablespoon baking powder
- 1/2 teaspoon salt
- 1/2 cup unsalted butter, cold and cut into small cubes
- 2/3 cup whole milk
- 1 teaspoon vanilla extract

For the Strawberries:

- 1 pound fresh strawberries, hulled and sliced
- 1/4 cup granulated sugar
- 1 teaspoon lemon juice

For the Whipped Cream:

- 1 cup heavy cream
- 2 tablespoons powdered sugar
- 1 teaspoon vanilla extract

Instructions:

Shortcakes:

    Preheat Oven:
- Preheat your oven to 425°F (220°C). Line a baking sheet with parchment paper.

    Mix Dry Ingredients:
- In a large bowl, whisk together the flour, sugar, baking powder, and salt.

    Cut in Butter:
- Add the cold, cubed butter to the dry ingredients. Use a pastry cutter or your fingers to cut the butter into the flour mixture until it resembles coarse crumbs.

    Add Wet Ingredients:

- Pour in the milk and vanilla extract. Stir until just combined. Do not overmix.

Form Dough:
- Turn the dough out onto a lightly floured surface and gently knead it a few times to bring it together. Pat the dough to about 1-inch thickness.

Cut Shortcakes:
- Use a round biscuit cutter to cut out shortcakes from the dough. Place them on the prepared baking sheet.

Bake:
- Bake in the preheated oven for 12-15 minutes or until the tops are golden brown. Allow the shortcakes to cool on a wire rack.

Strawberries:

Prepare Strawberries:
- In a bowl, combine the sliced strawberries, sugar, and lemon juice. Toss gently to coat the strawberries in sugar. Let them sit for about 15-20 minutes to release their juices.

Whipped Cream:

Whip Cream:
- In a separate bowl, whip the heavy cream, powdered sugar, and vanilla extract until stiff peaks form.

Assemble Strawberry Shortcakes:

Slice Shortcakes:
- Slice each shortcake in half horizontally.

Add Strawberries:
- Spoon a generous amount of strawberries onto the bottom half of each shortcake.

Top with Whipped Cream:
- Dollop a generous amount of whipped cream on top of the strawberries.

Place Top Half:
- Place the top half of the shortcake over the whipped cream.

Garnish (Optional):
- Garnish with additional strawberries or a dusting of powdered sugar if desired.

Serve:
- Serve these delicious Strawberry Shortcakes immediately and enjoy the perfect combination of sweet, juicy strawberries, fluffy shortcakes, and whipped cream!

Chocolate Turtles

Ingredients:

- 1 cup pecan halves
- 24 soft caramel candies, unwrapped
- 1 cup chocolate chips (semi-sweet or milk chocolate)
- Sea salt for sprinkling (optional)

Instructions:

Preheat Oven:
- Preheat your oven to 350°F (175°C). Line a baking sheet with parchment paper.

Toast Pecans:
- Spread the pecan halves in a single layer on the prepared baking sheet. Toast them in the preheated oven for about 8-10 minutes, stirring halfway through, until fragrant. Remove from the oven and let them cool.

Prepare Caramel Layer:
- While the pecans are toasting, place the unwrapped caramel candies in a heatproof bowl. Microwave them in 20-30 second intervals, stirring in between, until fully melted and smooth.

Assemble Turtles:
- Line another baking sheet with parchment paper. Arrange clusters of three toasted pecan halves on the parchment paper, forming the base for each turtle.
- Spoon a small amount of melted caramel over each cluster of pecans, ensuring the pecans stick together and are covered with caramel.
- Let the caramel set for a few minutes.

Melt Chocolate:
- In a microwave-safe bowl, melt the chocolate chips in 20-30 second intervals, stirring in between until smooth.

Coat Turtles:
- Spoon melted chocolate over each caramel and pecan cluster, covering them completely.

Chill:
- Place the turtles in the refrigerator for about 15-20 minutes to allow the chocolate to set.

Optional: Sea Salt:
- If desired, sprinkle a small amount of sea salt over the chocolate while it's still slightly soft.

Serve:
- Once the chocolate has set, remove the turtles from the refrigerator. Serve and enjoy these delicious homemade chocolate turtles!

Note:

- You can customize these turtles by adding a drizzle of white chocolate or sprinkling chopped nuts over the chocolate before it sets. Feel free to get creative with your toppings!

Dark Chocolate Avocado Mousse

Ingredients:

- 2 ripe avocados, peeled and pitted
- 1/2 cup dark cocoa powder
- 1/2 cup maple syrup or agave nectar
- 1 teaspoon vanilla extract
- 1/4 teaspoon salt
- 1/4 cup almond milk or any milk of your choice
- Optional toppings: fresh berries, chopped nuts, or whipped cream

Instructions:

Prepare Avocados:
- In a blender or food processor, combine the ripe avocados, dark cocoa powder, maple syrup (or agave nectar), vanilla extract, and salt.

Blend:
- Blend the ingredients until smooth and creamy. You may need to stop and scrape down the sides of the blender or food processor to ensure everything is well incorporated.

Add Milk:
- With the blender or food processor running, add the almond milk (or your chosen milk) gradually until you reach your desired mousse consistency. Add more milk if needed.

Adjust Sweetness:
- Taste the mousse and adjust the sweetness by adding more maple syrup or agave nectar if desired.

Chill:
- Transfer the dark chocolate avocado mousse to serving bowls or glasses. Cover and refrigerate for at least 30 minutes to chill and set.

Serve:
- Once chilled, you can serve the mousse as is or with your favorite toppings such as fresh berries, chopped nuts, or a dollop of whipped cream.

Enjoy:
- Enjoy this rich and creamy Dark Chocolate Avocado Mousse as a healthier alternative to traditional chocolate mousse!

Salted Caramel Brownies

Ingredients:

For the Brownies:

- 1 cup unsalted butter, melted
- 2 cups granulated sugar
- 4 large eggs
- 1 teaspoon vanilla extract
- 1 cup all-purpose flour
- 1/2 cup cocoa powder
- 1/4 teaspoon salt

For the Salted Caramel:

- 1 cup granulated sugar
- 6 tablespoons unsalted butter, cubed
- 1/2 cup heavy cream
- 1 teaspoon sea salt (or to taste)

Instructions:

Brownies:

Preheat Oven:
- Preheat your oven to 350°F (175°C). Grease and line a 9x13-inch baking pan with parchment paper.

Mix Wet Ingredients:
- In a large bowl, whisk together the melted butter and sugar until well combined.

Add Eggs and Vanilla:
- Add the eggs one at a time, beating well after each addition. Stir in the vanilla extract.

Combine Dry Ingredients:
- In a separate bowl, sift together the flour, cocoa powder, and salt.

Mix Batter:

- Gradually add the dry ingredients to the wet ingredients, mixing until just combined. Do not overmix.

Bake:
- Pour the brownie batter into the prepared baking pan. Smooth the top with a spatula. Bake in the preheated oven for 25-30 minutes or until a toothpick inserted into the center comes out with moist crumbs (not wet batter).

Cool:
- Allow the brownies to cool completely in the pan on a wire rack.

Salted Caramel:

Prepare Caramel Sauce:
- In a medium saucepan over medium heat, melt the granulated sugar, stirring constantly with a rubber spatula or wooden spoon.

Add Butter:
- Once the sugar has melted and turned amber in color, add the cubed butter. Stir until the butter is completely melted.

Slowly Add Cream:
- Carefully and slowly add the heavy cream while stirring constantly. Be cautious as the mixture will bubble up.

Simmer and Add Salt:
- Allow the caramel to simmer for 1-2 minutes, stirring continuously. Remove from heat and stir in the sea salt.

Cool:
- Let the salted caramel cool for a few minutes.

Assemble:

Drizzle Caramel:
- Once the brownies are completely cooled, drizzle the salted caramel over the top.

Chill (Optional):
- For cleaner slices, you can refrigerate the brownies for a few hours to allow the caramel to set.

Slice and Serve:
- Slice into squares and serve these indulgent Salted Caramel Brownies.

Enjoy:

- Enjoy the rich and gooey goodness of these delicious brownies with a perfect balance of chocolate and salted caramel!

Key Lime Pie

Ingredients:

For the Graham Cracker Crust:

- 1 1/2 cups graham cracker crumbs
- 1/3 cup granulated sugar
- 1/2 cup unsalted butter, melted

For the Key Lime Filling:

- 4 large egg yolks
- 2 cans (14 ounces each) sweetened condensed milk
- 1 cup freshly squeezed key lime juice (about 20-25 key limes)
- Zest of 1-2 key limes (optional)

For the Whipped Cream Topping:

- 1 cup heavy cream
- 2 tablespoons powdered sugar
- 1 teaspoon vanilla extract

Instructions:

Graham Cracker Crust:

   Preheat Oven:
   - Preheat your oven to 350°F (175°C).

   Combine Ingredients:
   - In a bowl, combine the graham cracker crumbs, granulated sugar, and melted butter. Mix until the crumbs are evenly coated.

   Press into Pan:
   - Press the mixture into the bottom and up the sides of a 9-inch pie pan to form the crust.

   Bake:

- Bake the crust in the preheated oven for about 10 minutes or until it is set. Allow it to cool while you prepare the filling.

Key Lime Filling:

Whisk Egg Yolks:
- In a mixing bowl, whisk the egg yolks until they are pale and slightly thickened.

Add Condensed Milk:
- Gradually add the sweetened condensed milk to the egg yolks, whisking continuously.

Add Lime Juice and Zest:
- Stir in the freshly squeezed key lime juice and zest (if using). Mix until well combined.

Pour into Crust:
- Pour the key lime filling into the cooled graham cracker crust.

Bake:
- Bake the pie in the preheated oven for about 15 minutes or until the edges are set, and the center is slightly jiggly.

Cool and Refrigerate:
- Allow the pie to cool to room temperature, then refrigerate for at least 4 hours or overnight to set.

Whipped Cream Topping:

Whip Cream:
- In a chilled bowl, whip the heavy cream, powdered sugar, and vanilla extract until stiff peaks form.

Top Pie:
- Spread or pipe the whipped cream over the chilled key lime pie.

Optional Garnish:
- Garnish with additional key lime zest or slices if desired.

Slice and Serve:
- Slice and serve this refreshing Key Lime Pie, savoring the perfect balance of sweet and tangy flavors!

Note:

- If key limes are not available, regular limes can be used as a substitute for both the juice and zest.

Mini Cheesecakes with Fruit Topping

Ingredients:

For the Cheesecake Base:

- 1 1/2 cups graham cracker crumbs
- 1/4 cup unsalted butter, melted
- 16 ounces cream cheese, softened
- 2/3 cup granulated sugar
- 2 large eggs
- 1 teaspoon vanilla extract
- 1/4 cup all-purpose flour
- 1/4 cup sour cream

For the Fruit Topping:

- Assorted fresh fruits (berries, kiwi, peaches, etc.)
- 1/4 cup fruit preserves or jelly (apricot or raspberry work well)
- 1 tablespoon water

Instructions:

Cheesecake Base:

  Preheat Oven:
  - Preheat your oven to 325°F (163°C). Line a muffin tin with paper liners.

  Make Crust:
  - In a bowl, combine the graham cracker crumbs and melted butter. Press a tablespoon of the mixture into the bottom of each paper-lined muffin cup to form the crust.

  Prepare Cream Cheese Mixture:
  - In a large mixing bowl, beat the softened cream cheese until smooth and creamy.

  Add Sugar:
  - Add the granulated sugar and continue to beat until well combined.

  Add Eggs and Vanilla:
  - Add the eggs, one at a time, beating well after each addition. Mix in the vanilla extract.

  Incorporate Flour and Sour Cream:

- Gently fold in the flour and sour cream until just combined. Do not overmix.

Fill Muffin Cups:
- Spoon the cream cheese mixture evenly over the crust in each muffin cup, filling almost to the top.

Bake:
- Bake in the preheated oven for about 18-20 minutes or until the centers are set.

Cool:
- Allow the mini cheesecakes to cool in the muffin tin for about 10 minutes, then transfer them to a wire rack to cool completely.

Fruit Topping:

Prepare Fruit:
- Wash and prepare the fresh fruits. Slice them into small pieces.

Make Glaze:
- In a small saucepan, heat the fruit preserves or jelly with 1 tablespoon of water over low heat. Stir until melted and smooth.

Assemble:
- Once the mini cheesecakes are cooled, spoon the melted fruit preserves or jelly over the top of each cheesecake.

Add Fresh Fruits:
- Arrange the sliced fresh fruits on top of the glaze.

Chill (Optional):
- For a firmer texture, you can refrigerate the mini cheesecakes for a few hours before serving.

Serve:
- Serve these delightful Mini Cheesecakes with Fruit Topping as a delightful and colorful dessert for any occasion!

Note:

- Feel free to mix and match the fruits based on your preference and what's in season.

Banana Foster

Ingredients:

- 4 ripe bananas, peeled and sliced
- 1/2 cup unsalted butter
- 1 cup brown sugar, packed
- 1/2 teaspoon ground cinnamon
- 1/4 cup banana liqueur
- 1/2 cup dark rum
- Vanilla ice cream for serving

Instructions:

Prepare Ingredients:
- Peel and slice the ripe bananas.

Melt Butter:
- In a large skillet over medium heat, melt the unsalted butter.

Add Brown Sugar and Cinnamon:
- Stir in the brown sugar and ground cinnamon, allowing the sugar to dissolve and the mixture to become smooth.

Add Bananas:
- Add the sliced bananas to the skillet, gently stirring to coat them in the caramel sauce.

Flambé with Banana Liqueur:
- Pour in the banana liqueur and carefully ignite it using a long lighter. Be cautious and stand back while it flames.

Simmer:
- Allow the flames to subside while the alcohol burns off. Let the mixture simmer for 1-2 minutes.

Add Dark Rum:
- Pour in the dark rum and, once again, ignite it using the long lighter. Be careful and stand back as it flames.

Stir and Serve:
- Gently stir the sauce until the flames subside. The sauce should be thick and glossy.

Serve with Ice Cream:
- Spoon the bananas and sauce over scoops of vanilla ice cream.

Enjoy:
- Serve immediately and enjoy this classic New Orleans dessert, Bananas Foster, with the warm, caramelized banana sauce over cool vanilla ice cream!

Note:

- Be cautious when working with flames, and keep a lid nearby to cover the skillet if needed. Adjust the quantity of rum and banana liqueur to suit your taste preferences.

Black Forest Cake

Ingredients:

For the Chocolate Cake:

- 1 and 3/4 cups all-purpose flour
- 2 cups granulated sugar
- 3/4 cup unsweetened cocoa powder
- 1 and 1/2 teaspoons baking powder
- 1 and 1/2 teaspoons baking soda
- 1 teaspoon salt
- 2 large eggs
- 1 cup whole milk
- 1/2 cup vegetable oil
- 2 teaspoons vanilla extract
- 1 cup boiling water

For the Cherry Filling:

- 1 can (24 ounces) cherry pie filling

For the Whipped Cream Frosting:

- 2 cups heavy cream, chilled
- 1/2 cup powdered sugar
- 1 teaspoon vanilla extract

For Garnish:

- Chocolate shavings
- Maraschino cherries

Instructions:

Chocolate Cake:

Preheat Oven:
- Preheat your oven to 350°F (175°C). Grease and flour two 9-inch round cake pans.

Combine Dry Ingredients:
- In a large bowl, whisk together the flour, sugar, cocoa powder, baking powder, baking soda, and salt.

Add Wet Ingredients:
- Add the eggs, milk, vegetable oil, and vanilla extract to the dry ingredients. Mix until well combined.

Add Boiling Water:
- Gradually add the boiling water to the batter, mixing until smooth. The batter will be thin.

Bake:
- Pour the batter evenly into the prepared pans. Bake in the preheated oven for 30-35 minutes or until a toothpick inserted into the center comes out clean.

Cool:
- Allow the cakes to cool in the pans for 10 minutes, then transfer them to a wire rack to cool completely.

Cherry Filling:

Prepare Cherries:
- Drain any excess liquid from the cherry pie filling.

Whipped Cream Frosting:

Whip Cream:
- In a chilled bowl, whip the heavy cream, powdered sugar, and vanilla extract until stiff peaks form.

Assemble the Black Forest Cake:

Slice Cakes:
- If the cakes have domed, level them using a serrated knife. Slice each cake in half horizontally, creating four layers in total.

Place First Layer:

- Place one cake layer on a serving plate. Spread a layer of whipped cream over the cake.

Add Cherries:
- Spoon a layer of cherry pie filling over the whipped cream.

Repeat Layers:
- Repeat the process with the remaining cake layers, whipped cream, and cherry filling.

Frost Top and Sides:
- Frost the top and sides of the cake with the remaining whipped cream.

Garnish:
- Garnish the top of the cake with chocolate shavings and maraschino cherries.

Chill (Optional):
- Refrigerate the Black Forest Cake for at least 1-2 hours before serving to allow the flavors to meld.

Slice and Serve:
- Slice and serve this classic Black Forest Cake, showcasing layers of moist chocolate cake, luscious whipped cream, and tart cherries.

Note:

- For an extra touch, you can brush each cake layer with a bit of Kirsch (cherry brandy) before adding the whipped cream and cherry filling.

Cherry Almond Clafoutis

Ingredients:

- 1 cup cherries, pitted
- 1/2 cup slivered almonds
- 3 large eggs
- 1/2 cup granulated sugar
- 1 cup whole milk
- 1/2 cup all-purpose flour
- 1/4 cup almond flour
- 1 teaspoon almond extract
- 1/2 teaspoon vanilla extract
- 1/4 teaspoon salt
- Powdered sugar for dusting (optional)

Instructions:

Preheat Oven:
- Preheat your oven to 350°F (175°C). Grease a baking dish (about 9 inches in diameter) with butter or non-stick spray.

Prepare Cherries:
- Wash and pit the cherries. You can leave them whole or cut them in half.

Spread Cherries and Almonds:
- Spread the cherries and slivered almonds evenly in the bottom of the prepared baking dish.

Mix Batter:
- In a blender or mixing bowl, combine the eggs, granulated sugar, whole milk, all-purpose flour, almond flour, almond extract, vanilla extract, and salt. Blend or whisk until the batter is smooth.

Pour Batter Over Cherries:
- Pour the batter over the cherries and almonds in the baking dish.

Bake:
- Bake in the preheated oven for 40-45 minutes or until the clafoutis is puffed, set in the center, and golden brown on the edges.

Cool Slightly:
- Allow the clafoutis to cool slightly before serving. It will deflate a bit as it cools.

Dust with Powdered Sugar:

- Dust the top of the clafoutis with powdered sugar before serving, if desired.

Serve Warm:
- Serve the Cherry Almond Clafoutis warm, either on its own or with a dollop of whipped cream or a scoop of vanilla ice cream.

Enjoy:
- Enjoy the delightful combination of juicy cherries, crunchy almonds, and the almond-infused custard in this classic French dessert!

Note:

- Traditional clafoutis is made with unpitted cherries to enhance the flavor, but you can pit them if you prefer. The almond flour adds a subtle nuttiness to the dish, but you can use all-purpose flour if almond flour is not available.

Almond Joy Truffles

Ingredients:

- 1 cup sweetened shredded coconut
- 1/2 cup sweetened condensed milk
- 1/2 cup slivered almonds, toasted
- 1/2 cup milk chocolate chips
- 1/2 teaspoon vanilla extract
- Pinch of salt
- Additional shredded coconut for rolling (optional)
- Additional chocolate for drizzling (optional)

Instructions:

Toast Almonds:
- In a dry skillet over medium heat, toast the slivered almonds until golden brown. Stir frequently to prevent burning. Remove from heat and let them cool.

Blend Mixture:
- In a food processor, combine the toasted almonds, sweetened shredded coconut, sweetened condensed milk, chocolate chips, vanilla extract, and a pinch of salt. Pulse until the mixture comes together and is well combined.

Chill Mixture:
- Transfer the mixture to a bowl and refrigerate for about 15-30 minutes to firm up slightly, making it easier to handle.

Shape Truffles:
- Once the mixture has chilled, take small portions and roll them into bite-sized balls. If desired, roll the truffles in additional shredded coconut for an extra coating.

Chill Again:
- Place the shaped truffles on a parchment-lined tray and refrigerate for at least 1 hour to firm up.

Optional Chocolate Drizzle:
- If you want to add a chocolate drizzle, melt some additional chocolate (milk or dark) and drizzle it over the chilled truffles.

Chill Until Set:

- Return the truffles to the refrigerator until the chocolate drizzle is set.

Serve and Enjoy:
- Once fully set, these Almond Joy Truffles are ready to be served. Enjoy the delightful combination of coconut, almonds, and chocolate in each bite!

Note:

- Feel free to adjust the sweetness by adding more or less sweetened condensed milk according to your taste preferences.

Lemon Bars

Ingredients:

For the Shortbread Crust:

- 1 cup unsalted butter, softened
- 1/2 cup granulated sugar
- 2 cups all-purpose flour
- 1/4 teaspoon salt

For the Lemon Filling:

- 4 large eggs
- 1 and 1/2 cups granulated sugar
- 1/3 cup all-purpose flour
- 1 cup freshly squeezed lemon juice (about 4-6 lemons)
- Zest of 1-2 lemons
- Powdered sugar for dusting (optional)

Instructions:

Shortbread Crust:

Preheat Oven:
- Preheat your oven to 350°F (175°C). Grease a 9x13-inch baking dish or line it with parchment paper.

Cream Butter and Sugar:
- In a mixing bowl, cream together the softened butter and granulated sugar until light and fluffy.

Add Flour and Salt:
- Add the flour and salt to the creamed mixture. Mix until just combined. The dough will be crumbly.

Press into Pan:
- Press the shortbread dough evenly into the bottom of the prepared baking dish.

Bake:

- Bake the crust in the preheated oven for about 20-25 minutes or until it is lightly golden brown.

Lemon Filling:

Prepare Lemon Juice and Zest:
- While the crust is baking, prepare the lemon juice and zest.

Whisk Eggs and Sugar:
- In a bowl, whisk together the eggs and granulated sugar until well combined.

Add Flour:
- Gradually add the flour to the egg and sugar mixture, whisking continuously to avoid lumps.

Add Lemon Juice and Zest:
- Stir in the freshly squeezed lemon juice and lemon zest. Mix until smooth.

Pour over Baked Crust:
- Pour the lemon filling over the baked shortbread crust while it is still warm.

Bake Again:
- Return the pan to the oven and bake for an additional 20-25 minutes or until the lemon filling is set and no longer jiggles.

Cool:
- Allow the lemon bars to cool in the baking dish. Once cooled, refrigerate for at least 2 hours to firm up.

Dust with Powdered Sugar:
- Before serving, dust the top with powdered sugar if desired.

Cut and Serve:
- Cut into squares and serve these tangy and sweet Lemon Bars.

Note:

- Adjust the amount of sugar in the filling according to your taste preference. If you prefer a more tart flavor, you can reduce the sugar slightly.

Chocolate Raspberry Tart

Ingredients:

For the Chocolate Tart Shell:

- 1 and 1/4 cups all-purpose flour
- 1/4 cup cocoa powder
- 1/2 cup unsalted butter, chilled and diced
- 1/4 cup granulated sugar
- 1 large egg yolk
- 2 tablespoons cold water

For the Chocolate Ganache Filling:

- 8 ounces dark chocolate, finely chopped
- 1 cup heavy cream
- 2 tablespoons unsalted butter

For the Raspberry Topping:

- 1 and 1/2 cups fresh raspberries
- 1/4 cup raspberry jam, melted (for glazing)

Instructions:

Chocolate Tart Shell:

    Preheat Oven:
- Preheat your oven to 350°F (175°C).

    Prepare Tart Dough:
- In a food processor, combine the flour, cocoa powder, chilled diced butter, and granulated sugar. Pulse until the mixture resembles coarse crumbs.

    Add Egg Yolk and Water:
- Add the egg yolk and cold water. Pulse again until the dough starts to come together.

    Form Dough:
- Turn the dough out onto a lightly floured surface and knead it gently until it forms a smooth ball.

    Roll Out Dough:

- Roll out the dough into a circle large enough to fit your tart pan.

Transfer to Tart Pan:
- Carefully transfer the rolled-out dough to a 9-inch tart pan with a removable bottom. Press the dough into the bottom and up the sides of the pan.

Chill:
- Place the tart shell in the refrigerator and chill for at least 30 minutes.

Bake:
- Once chilled, bake the tart shell in the preheated oven for about 15-18 minutes or until it is set. Allow it to cool completely.

Chocolate Ganache Filling:

Prepare Chocolate:
- Place the finely chopped dark chocolate in a heatproof bowl.

Heat Cream:
- In a small saucepan, heat the heavy cream until it just begins to simmer.

Pour Over Chocolate:
- Pour the hot cream over the chopped chocolate. Let it sit for a minute, then stir until smooth and well combined.

Add Butter:
- Stir in the unsalted butter until it is fully melted and incorporated into the chocolate.

Fill Tart Shell:
- Pour the chocolate ganache into the cooled tart shell. Smooth the top with a spatula.

Chill:
- Refrigerate the tart for at least 2 hours or until the ganache is set.

Raspberry Topping:

Arrange Raspberries:
- Arrange fresh raspberries on top of the chilled chocolate ganache.

Glaze with Jam:
- Heat the raspberry jam until it becomes liquid. Brush the melted jam over the top of the raspberries for a glossy finish.

Chill Again:
- Return the tart to the refrigerator for about 30 minutes to set the glaze.

Slice and Serve:

- Slice and serve this decadent Chocolate Raspberry Tart for a delightful combination of rich chocolate and vibrant raspberries.

Note:

- You can customize the tart by using a mix of dark and milk chocolate for the ganache or adding a layer of raspberry coulis before pouring the chocolate ganache.

Cinnamon Sugar Churros

Ingredients:

For the Churro Dough:

- 1 cup water
- 1/2 cup unsalted butter
- 2 tablespoons granulated sugar
- 1/2 teaspoon salt
- 1 cup all-purpose flour
- 3 large eggs
- Vegetable oil, for frying

For the Cinnamon Sugar Coating:

- 1/2 cup granulated sugar
- 1 teaspoon ground cinnamon

Instructions:

Churro Dough:

    Prepare Dough:
- In a saucepan, combine water, butter, sugar, and salt. Bring to a boil over medium heat.

    Add Flour:
- Once boiling, reduce heat to low and add the flour. Stir vigorously with a wooden spoon until the mixture forms a smooth dough. Remove from heat.

    Add Eggs:
- Let the dough cool for a few minutes, then add the eggs one at a time, stirring well after each addition. The dough should be smooth and glossy.

    Heat Oil:
- Heat vegetable oil in a deep saucepan or fryer to 375°F (190°C).

    Pipe Churros:

- Transfer the churro dough to a piping bag fitted with a star tip. Pipe 4-6 inch strips of dough directly into the hot oil, using scissors or a knife to cut the dough.

Fry Churros:
- Fry the churros until golden brown, turning them occasionally for even cooking. This takes about 2-4 minutes per batch.

Drain on Paper Towels:
- Remove the churros with a slotted spoon and drain them on paper towels.

Cinnamon Sugar Coating:

Mix Sugar and Cinnamon:
- In a bowl, combine granulated sugar and ground cinnamon.

Coat Churros:
- While the churros are still warm, roll them in the cinnamon sugar mixture until well coated.

Serve Warm:
- Serve the Cinnamon Sugar Churros warm and enjoy their crispy exterior and soft interior.

Optional: Chocolate Sauce for Dipping

- Melted chocolate or chocolate sauce for dipping.

Note:

- Adjust the size of the churros according to your preference.
- Feel free to serve with a side of melted chocolate or chocolate sauce for dipping.

Coconut Macaroons

Ingredients:

- 3 cups shredded coconut (sweetened)
- 3/4 cup sweetened condensed milk
- 1 teaspoon vanilla extract
- 2 large egg whites
- 1/4 teaspoon salt
- Optional: 1 cup chocolate chips or melted chocolate for dipping

Instructions:

Preheat Oven:
- Preheat your oven to 325°F (163°C). Line a baking sheet with parchment paper.

Combine Ingredients:
- In a large mixing bowl, combine the shredded coconut, sweetened condensed milk, and vanilla extract. Mix until well combined.

Whip Egg Whites:
- In a separate bowl, whip the egg whites and salt until stiff peaks form.

Fold in Egg Whites:
- Gently fold the whipped egg whites into the coconut mixture until evenly combined. Be careful not to deflate the egg whites.

Shape Macaroons:
- Using a spoon or cookie scoop, drop rounded mounds of the coconut mixture onto the prepared baking sheet. Space them about 2 inches apart.

Bake:
- Bake in the preheated oven for 15-18 minutes or until the edges are golden brown.

Cool:
- Allow the coconut macaroons to cool on the baking sheet for a few minutes before transferring them to a wire rack to cool completely.

Optional: Dip in Chocolate:
- If desired, melt chocolate chips or chocolate and dip the bottoms of the cooled macaroons into the chocolate. Place them back on the parchment paper to let the chocolate set.

Serve:

- Once the chocolate is set, serve these delicious Coconut Macaroons. Enjoy their sweet and chewy texture!

Note:

- You can customize these macaroons by adding ingredients like chopped nuts or dried fruit to the coconut mixture.
- Adjust the baking time for your desired level of crispiness. Longer baking times will result in a crunchier exterior.

Pistachio Ice Cream

Ingredients:

- 2 cups shelled pistachios (unsalted)
- 2 cups whole milk
- 2 cups heavy cream
- 1 cup granulated sugar
- 1 teaspoon vanilla extract
- A pinch of salt

Instructions:

Prepare the Pistachios:
- If your pistachios are not already shelled, remove the shells to get 2 cups of shelled pistachios.
- You can either use raw pistachios or lightly roast them for enhanced flavor. Allow them to cool before using.

Blend the Pistachios:
- In a food processor or blender, pulse the pistachios until they are finely ground. Be careful not to over-process; you want a slightly coarse texture for added crunch in the ice cream.

Make the Ice Cream Base:
- In a saucepan, combine the milk, heavy cream, sugar, vanilla extract, and a pinch of salt.
- Heat the mixture over medium heat until it is warm but not boiling, stirring to dissolve the sugar.

Infuse Pistachio Flavor:
- Add the ground pistachios to the warm milk and cream mixture.
- Continue to heat the mixture over low-medium heat, stirring constantly, for about 10-15 minutes. This allows the pistachio flavor to infuse into the liquid.

Strain the Mixture:
- Strain the mixture through a fine-mesh sieve or cheesecloth to remove the larger pieces of pistachio. Press down on the solids to extract as much flavor as possible.

Chill the Mixture:
- Refrigerate the strained mixture until it is thoroughly chilled. This usually takes a few hours or overnight.

Churn the Ice Cream:
- Once chilled, transfer the mixture to an ice cream maker and churn according to the manufacturer's instructions.

Freeze:
- Transfer the churned ice cream to a lidded container and freeze for a few hours or until it reaches your desired consistency.

Serve and Enjoy:
- Scoop the pistachio ice cream into bowls or cones and enjoy the creamy, nutty goodness!

Feel free to customize the recipe to suit your taste preferences, and you can even add chopped pistachios or chocolate chips during the last few minutes of churning for added texture.

Mocha Pots de Creme

Ingredients:

- 2 cups heavy cream
- 1/2 cup whole milk
- 1/2 cup granulated sugar
- 1/4 cup unsweetened cocoa powder
- 4 ounces high-quality dark chocolate, chopped
- 2 tablespoons instant coffee or espresso powder
- 6 large egg yolks
- 1 teaspoon vanilla extract
- A pinch of salt
- Whipped cream and chocolate shavings for garnish (optional)

Instructions:

Preheat Oven:
- Preheat your oven to 325°F (163°C).

Prepare Ramekins:
- Arrange 6 to 8 ramekins or small jars in a baking dish. Set aside.

Heat Cream and Milk:
- In a saucepan, combine the heavy cream, whole milk, sugar, cocoa powder, chopped chocolate, and instant coffee or espresso powder. Heat over medium heat, stirring constantly, until the mixture is hot and the chocolate is completely melted.

Whisk Egg Yolks:
- In a separate bowl, whisk the egg yolks until well beaten.

Temper the Eggs:
- Slowly pour a small amount of the hot chocolate mixture into the beaten egg yolks, whisking continuously. This helps to temper the eggs and prevent them from curdling.

Combine Mixtures:
- Gradually add the tempered egg mixture back into the saucepan with the remaining hot chocolate mixture, stirring constantly.

Add Vanilla and Salt:
- Stir in the vanilla extract and a pinch of salt. Continue to heat the mixture until it thickens slightly, but do not let it boil.

Strain the Mixture:

- Strain the mixture through a fine-mesh sieve or cheesecloth into a bowl or pitcher to remove any lumps or egg bits.

Fill Ramekins:
- Pour the mixture evenly into the prepared ramekins or jars.

Create Water Bath:
- Place the baking dish with the filled ramekins in the preheated oven. Pour hot water into the baking dish to create a water bath, reaching halfway up the sides of the ramekins.

Bake:
- Bake for about 30-40 minutes or until the pots de crème are set around the edges but still slightly jiggly in the center.

Cool and Chill:
- Allow the pots de crème to cool in the water bath before transferring them to the refrigerator. Chill for at least 4 hours or overnight.

Serve:
- Before serving, you can garnish each pot de crème with a dollop of whipped cream and chocolate shavings if desired.

Enjoy this decadent Mocha Pots de Crème with its velvety texture and rich coffee-chocolate flavor!

Chocolate Dipped Pretzels

Ingredients:

- Pretzels (large or small pretzel twists or rods)
- Chocolate (dark, milk, or white chocolate, depending on your preference)
- Toppings for decoration (optional): sprinkles, crushed nuts, shredded coconut, etc.

Instructions:

Prepare Pretzels:
- Select your desired pretzels. You can use small twists, rods, or any shape you like. Lay them out on a parchment paper-lined baking sheet or tray.

Melt the Chocolate:
- Chop the chocolate into small, uniform pieces for easy melting.
- In a heatproof bowl, melt the chocolate using one of these methods:
    - Microwave: Heat in 20-second intervals, stirring between each, until smooth.
    - Double Boiler: Place the bowl over a pot of simmering water, ensuring the water doesn't touch the bottom of the bowl. Stir until melted.

Dip Pretzels:
- Hold a pretzel by one end and dip it into the melted chocolate, covering about two-thirds of the pretzel. Use a spoon or spatula to help coat the pretzel evenly.

Tap Off Excess Chocolate:
- Gently tap the chocolate-dipped pretzel against the side of the bowl to remove any excess chocolate.

Add Toppings (Optional):
- If you want to add toppings like sprinkles, crushed nuts, or shredded coconut, do so while the chocolate is still wet.

Place on Parchment Paper:
- Lay the chocolate-dipped pretzels on a parchment paper-lined tray or baking sheet, ensuring they are not touching each other.

Let Chocolate Set:
- Allow the chocolate to set. You can speed up the process by placing the tray in the refrigerator for about 15-20 minutes.

Store:
- Once the chocolate has completely set, transfer the chocolate-dipped pretzels to an airtight container. Store in a cool, dry place.

Serve:
- Enjoy the chocolate-dipped pretzels on their own or use them as a sweet and salty addition to party platters or dessert tables.

These chocolate-dipped pretzels make for a versatile and crowd-pleasing snack. You can get creative with different chocolate types and toppings to suit your taste preferences.

Bourbon Pecan Pie

Ingredients:

For the Pie Crust:

- 1 1/4 cups all-purpose flour
- 1/2 cup unsalted butter, cold and cut into small pieces
- 1/4 teaspoon salt
- 2-3 tablespoons ice water

For the Filling:

- 1 cup granulated sugar
- 1 cup light corn syrup
- 1/2 cup unsalted butter, melted
- 4 large eggs, lightly beaten
- 1/4 cup bourbon
- 1 teaspoon vanilla extract
- 1/4 teaspoon salt
- 2 cups pecan halves

Instructions:

For the Pie Crust:

Prepare the Dough:
- In a food processor, combine the flour and salt. Add the cold, diced butter and pulse until the mixture resembles coarse crumbs.
- With the processor running, gradually add ice water, one tablespoon at a time, until the dough just comes together.
- Turn the dough out onto a lightly floured surface, knead it a few times to bring it together, then shape it into a disk. Wrap in plastic wrap and refrigerate for at least 1 hour.

Roll Out the Crust:
- Preheat your oven to 375°F (190°C).
- Roll out the chilled dough on a floured surface to fit a 9-inch pie dish. Place the rolled-out crust into the pie dish, trim the excess, and crimp the edges. Place the pie crust in the refrigerator while you prepare the filling.

For the Filling:

Mix the Filling:
- In a large mixing bowl, whisk together sugar, corn syrup, melted butter, beaten eggs, bourbon, vanilla extract, and salt until well combined.

Add Pecans:
- Stir in the pecan halves until evenly coated with the filling mixture.

Fill the Pie Crust:
- Take the pie crust out of the refrigerator and pour the pecan filling into it.

Bake:
- Place the pie on a baking sheet to catch any spills and bake in the preheated oven for 40-50 minutes or until the center is set. You can cover the edges of the crust with foil if they start to brown too quickly.

Cool:
- Allow the Bourbon Pecan Pie to cool completely on a wire rack before slicing.

Serve:
- Serve the pie at room temperature or slightly warmed, and optionally, top with a dollop of whipped cream or a scoop of vanilla ice cream.

Enjoy the delightful combination of rich pecan filling with a hint of bourbon in this classic Southern Bourbon Pecan Pie!

Mango Sorbet

Ingredients:

- 4 cups ripe mango, peeled, pitted, and diced (about 4-5 medium-sized mangoes)
- 1 cup granulated sugar (adjust according to your sweetness preference and the sweetness of the mangoes)
- 1/4 cup freshly squeezed lime or lemon juice
- 1 cup water

Instructions:

Prepare the Mango:
- Peel, pit, and dice the ripe mangoes.

Make Simple Syrup:
- In a small saucepan, combine the sugar and water. Heat over medium heat, stirring until the sugar is completely dissolved. Remove from heat and let the simple syrup cool to room temperature.

Blend Mangoes:
- In a blender or food processor, puree the diced mangoes until smooth.

Combine Ingredients:
- In a bowl, combine the mango puree, cooled simple syrup, and lime or lemon juice. Stir well to ensure even mixing.

Strain (Optional):
- If you prefer a smoother sorbet, you can strain the mixture through a fine-mesh sieve or cheesecloth to remove any fibrous bits. This step is optional, as some people enjoy the texture of the mango fibers.

Chill the Mixture:
- Refrigerate the mango mixture for at least 2-3 hours or until it's thoroughly chilled. This step helps the sorbet freeze more quickly and efficiently.

Freeze:
- Transfer the chilled mixture to an ice cream maker and churn according to the manufacturer's instructions until it reaches a sorbet-like consistency.

Transfer to a Container:
- Transfer the churned sorbet to a lidded container.

Final Freeze:
- Freeze the mango sorbet for an additional 3-4 hours or until it reaches your desired firmness.

Serve:

- Scoop the mango sorbet into bowls or cones and enjoy its smooth and tropical flavor.

Feel free to customize the recipe by adding a splash of coconut milk for a tropical twist or experimenting with other complementary flavors. Mango sorbet is a delightful dairy-free option that captures the natural sweetness of ripe mangoes.

Oreo Cheesecake Bites

Ingredients:

For the Crust:

- 1 1/2 cups crushed Oreo cookies (with cream filling), about 15-18 cookies
- 1/4 cup unsalted butter, melted

For the Cheesecake Filling:

- 2 cups cream cheese, softened
- 1/2 cup granulated sugar
- 2 large eggs
- 1 teaspoon vanilla extract
- 1/2 cup sour cream
- 1/2 cup crushed Oreo cookies (optional, for added texture)

For Topping:

- Additional crushed Oreo cookies for garnish (optional)

Instructions:

Preheat the Oven:
- Preheat your oven to 325°F (163°C). Line a mini muffin tin with paper liners.

Make the Oreo Crust:
- In a bowl, mix the crushed Oreo cookies with melted butter until well combined.
- Place a tablespoon of the Oreo mixture into each mini muffin cup. Press down with the back of a spoon to create a compact crust.

Prepare Cheesecake Filling:
- In a large bowl, beat the softened cream cheese until smooth using an electric mixer.
- Add sugar and continue beating until well combined.
- Add eggs one at a time, beating well after each addition.

- Mix in the vanilla extract and sour cream until the batter is smooth.
- Optionally, fold in the crushed Oreo cookies for added texture.

Fill the Muffin Cups:
- Spoon the cheesecake filling over the Oreo crusts in the mini muffin cups, filling each nearly to the top.

Bake:
- Bake in the preheated oven for about 15-18 minutes or until the cheesecake bites are set and a toothpick inserted into the center comes out clean.

Cool:
- Allow the Oreo cheesecake bites to cool in the muffin tin for a few minutes before transferring them to a wire rack to cool completely.

Chill:
- Once cooled, refrigerate the cheesecake bites for at least 2-3 hours or overnight to firm up.

Serve:
- Optionally, garnish each Oreo cheesecake bite with additional crushed Oreo cookies before serving.

These Oreo cheesecake bites are a delightful treat for Oreo and cheesecake lovers alike.

They make for a perfect bite-sized dessert for parties or gatherings. Enjoy!

Maple Pecan Blondies

Ingredients:

- 1 cup unsalted butter, melted
- 2 cups light brown sugar, packed
- 2 large eggs
- 1 tablespoon vanilla extract
- 1/4 cup pure maple syrup
- 2 cups all-purpose flour
- 1 teaspoon baking powder
- 1/2 teaspoon salt
- 1 cup chopped pecans

Instructions:

Preheat the Oven:
- Preheat your oven to 350°F (175°C). Grease and flour a 9x13-inch baking pan or line it with parchment paper.

Melt Butter:
- In a microwave-safe bowl or using a stovetop, melt the butter. Allow it to cool slightly.

Mix Wet Ingredients:
- In a large mixing bowl, combine the melted butter and packed brown sugar. Stir until well combined.
- Add the eggs one at a time, beating well after each addition.
- Mix in the vanilla extract and pure maple syrup until the mixture is smooth.

Combine Dry Ingredients:
- In a separate bowl, whisk together the flour, baking powder, and salt.

Combine Wet and Dry Ingredients:
- Gradually add the dry ingredients to the wet ingredients, mixing until just combined. Avoid overmixing.

Add Pecans:
- Gently fold in the chopped pecans until evenly distributed in the batter.

Spread Batter in the Pan:
- Spread the blondie batter evenly into the prepared baking pan.

Bake:

- Bake in the preheated oven for about 25-30 minutes or until a toothpick inserted into the center comes out with a few moist crumbs. Be careful not to overbake, as you want the blondies to be moist and chewy.

Cool:
- Allow the maple pecan blondies to cool in the pan for about 15 minutes before transferring them to a wire rack to cool completely.

Slice and Serve:
- Once cooled, cut the blondies into squares or bars. They can be served as is or dusted with powdered sugar for an extra touch.

These maple pecan blondies are a delightful treat with the perfect combination of sweet maple flavor and the nutty crunch of pecans. Enjoy them with a cup of coffee or as a dessert for any occasion!

Peach Cobbler

Ingredients:

For the Blondies:

- 1 cup unsalted butter, melted
- 2 cups light brown sugar, packed
- 2 large eggs
- 1 tablespoon vanilla extract
- 2 cups all-purpose flour
- 1/2 teaspoon baking powder
- 1/4 teaspoon baking soda
- 1/2 teaspoon salt
- 1 cup chopped pecans

For the Maple Glaze:

- 1/2 cup unsalted butter
- 1 cup confectioners' sugar
- 2 tablespoons pure maple syrup
- 1 teaspoon vanilla extract

Instructions:

Preheat the Oven:
- Preheat your oven to 350°F (175°C). Grease a 9x13-inch baking dish and line it with parchment paper, leaving an overhang for easy removal.

Make the Blondie Batter:
- In a large bowl, whisk together the melted butter and brown sugar until well combined.
- Add the eggs and vanilla extract, and whisk until smooth.

Add Dry Ingredients:
- In a separate bowl, whisk together the flour, baking powder, baking soda, and salt.
- Gradually add the dry ingredients to the wet ingredients, mixing until just combined.

- Fold in the chopped pecans.

Spread Batter in the Pan:
- Spread the blondie batter evenly into the prepared baking dish.

Bake:
- Bake in the preheated oven for 25-30 minutes or until a toothpick inserted into the center comes out with moist crumbs but not wet batter.

Make the Maple Glaze:
- While the blondies are baking, prepare the maple glaze. In a small saucepan, melt the butter over medium heat.
- Add confectioners' sugar, maple syrup, and vanilla extract. Whisk until smooth and well combined.

Glaze the Blondies:
- Once the blondies are done baking, let them cool for about 10 minutes in the pan.
- Pour the warm maple glaze over the slightly cooled blondies, spreading it evenly.

Cool and Slice:
- Allow the blondies to cool completely in the pan before lifting them out using the parchment paper overhang. Place them on a cutting board and slice into squares.

Serve:
- Serve the Maple Pecan Blondies and enjoy the delightful combination of sweet maple and crunchy pecans.

These blondies are a perfect treat for any occasion, and the maple glaze adds an extra layer of flavor that elevates them to a new level of deliciousness.

Cannoli

Ingredients:

For the Cannoli Shells:

- 2 cups all-purpose flour
- 2 tablespoons granulated sugar
- 1/4 teaspoon salt
- 2 tablespoons unsalted butter, cold and cut into small pieces
- 1 cup white wine or Marsala wine
- Vegetable oil, for frying

For the Ricotta Filling:

- 2 cups whole milk ricotta cheese, drained
- 1 cup confectioners' sugar
- 1 teaspoon vanilla extract
- 1/3 cup mini chocolate chips
- 1/4 cup chopped pistachios (optional)
- Additional confectioners' sugar, for dusting

Instructions:

For the Cannoli Shells:

Make the Dough:
- In a large bowl, whisk together the flour, sugar, and salt. Add the cold butter pieces and incorporate them into the flour mixture using your fingers until the mixture resembles coarse crumbs.
- Gradually add the wine, mixing until a dough forms.

Knead and Rest the Dough:
- Turn the dough onto a lightly floured surface and knead it until smooth. Wrap the dough in plastic wrap and let it rest at room temperature for at least 30 minutes.

Roll and Cut the Shells:

- Roll out the dough on a floured surface until it's very thin. Using a round cutter or a glass, cut out circles from the dough.

Wrap Around Cannoli Tubes:
- Wrap each circle of dough around a cannoli tube, sealing the edges with a bit of beaten egg or water.

Fry the Shells:
- Heat vegetable oil in a large, deep pot to 350°F (175°C).
- Fry the cannoli shells a few at a time until golden brown and crispy. Remove them with tongs and place them on paper towels to drain excess oil. Let the shells cool before removing the tubes.

For the Ricotta Filling:

Prepare the Filling:
- In a bowl, mix together the drained ricotta cheese, confectioners' sugar, and vanilla extract until smooth and creamy.

Add Chocolate Chips:
- Fold in the mini chocolate chips (and chopped pistachios if using).

Assembling the Cannoli:

Fill the Cannoli Shells:
- Using a pastry bag or a zip-top bag with the corner cut off, pipe the ricotta filling into both ends of each cannoli shell.

Optional Garnish:
- Optionally, dip the ends of the filled cannoli into additional mini chocolate chips or chopped pistachios.

Dust with Confectioners' Sugar:
- Dust the filled cannoli with confectioners' sugar just before serving.

Enjoy these homemade cannoli with their crispy shells and creamy ricotta filling—a delightful Italian dessert!

Dark Chocolate and Sea Salt Caramel Tart

Ingredients:

For the Chocolate Tart Shell:

- 1 1/2 cups all-purpose flour
- 1/2 cup unsweetened cocoa powder
- 1/2 cup confectioners' sugar
- 1/4 teaspoon salt
- 1 cup unsalted butter, cold and cut into small cubes
- 1 large egg yolk
- 2 tablespoons ice water

For the Caramel Filling:

- 1 cup granulated sugar
- 1/4 cup water
- 1/2 cup heavy cream
- 4 tablespoons unsalted butter
- 1 teaspoon sea salt (plus extra for garnish)

For the Dark Chocolate Ganache:

- 8 ounces dark chocolate, finely chopped
- 1 cup heavy cream

Instructions:

For the Chocolate Tart Shell:

Prepare the Dough:
- In a food processor, combine the flour, cocoa powder, confectioners' sugar, and salt. Pulse to mix.
- Add the cold, cubed butter, and pulse until the mixture resembles coarse crumbs.

- In a small bowl, mix the egg yolk with ice water. Add it to the processor and pulse until the dough just comes together.

Form the Tart Shell:
- Turn the dough out onto a lightly floured surface and gather it into a ball. Flatten into a disk, wrap in plastic wrap, and refrigerate for at least 30 minutes.

Roll Out and Bake:
- Preheat your oven to 375°F (190°C).
- Roll out the chilled dough on a floured surface and fit it into a tart pan. Trim any excess dough.
- Prick the bottom with a fork and line with parchment paper. Fill with pie weights or dried beans.
- Bake for 15 minutes. Remove the weights and parchment paper, then bake for an additional 10 minutes or until the crust is set. Let it cool.

For the Caramel Filling:

Make the Caramel:
- In a heavy saucepan, combine granulated sugar and water over medium heat. Stir until the sugar dissolves, then let it boil without stirring.
- Cook until the mixture turns a deep amber color. Remove from heat and carefully add the heavy cream, butter, and sea salt. Stir until smooth.

Pour into Tart Shell:
- Pour the caramel into the cooled tart shell. Let it cool and set while you prepare the chocolate ganache.

For the Dark Chocolate Ganache:

Prepare Ganache:
- Place the finely chopped dark chocolate in a heatproof bowl.
- In a small saucepan, heat the cream until it just starts to simmer. Pour it over the chocolate.
- Let it sit for a minute, then stir until the chocolate is melted and the ganache is smooth.

Pour Over Caramel:
- Pour the dark chocolate ganache over the set caramel layer in the tart shell. Smooth the top with a spatula.

Chill:

- Refrigerate the tart for at least 2-3 hours or until the chocolate ganache is set.

Serve:
- Before serving, sprinkle a little sea salt over the top for added flavor.

Enjoy this luxurious Dark Chocolate and Sea Salt Caramel Tart for a delightful and indulgent dessert!

Strawberry Tiramisu

Ingredients:

For the Strawberry Sauce:

- 2 cups fresh strawberries, hulled and sliced
- 1/4 cup granulated sugar
- 1 tablespoon lemon juice

For the Tiramisu:

- 1 cup heavy cream
- 1 cup mascarpone cheese
- 1/2 cup confectioners' sugar
- 1 teaspoon vanilla extract
- 1 cup strong brewed coffee, cooled
- 3 tablespoons coffee liqueur (optional)
- Ladyfinger cookies (about 24)
- Cocoa powder, for dusting
- Fresh strawberries for garnish

Instructions:

For the Strawberry Sauce:

Prepare Strawberry Sauce:
- In a saucepan, combine the sliced strawberries, granulated sugar, and lemon juice.
- Cook over medium heat until the strawberries break down and the mixture thickens, stirring occasionally. Remove from heat and let it cool.

For the Tiramisu:

Prepare Coffee Mixture:
- Mix the brewed coffee and coffee liqueur (if using) in a shallow dish.

Make Mascarpone Mixture:

- In a large bowl, whip the heavy cream until stiff peaks form.
- In another bowl, whisk together the mascarpone cheese, confectioners' sugar, and vanilla extract until smooth.
- Gently fold the whipped cream into the mascarpone mixture until well combined.

Assemble Tiramisu:
- Dip each ladyfinger into the coffee mixture briefly, making sure not to soak them too much.
- Arrange a layer of dipped ladyfingers in the bottom of a serving dish or individual glasses.

Add Strawberry Layer:
- Spoon a layer of the strawberry sauce over the ladyfingers.

Add Mascarpone Layer:
- Spread half of the mascarpone mixture over the strawberry layer.

Repeat Layers:
- Repeat the layers with another layer of dipped ladyfingers, strawberry sauce, and the remaining mascarpone mixture.

Chill:
- Cover and refrigerate the Strawberry Tiramisu for at least 4 hours or overnight to allow the flavors to meld and the dessert to set.

Dust with Cocoa Powder:
- Before serving, dust the top with cocoa powder.

Garnish and Serve:
- Garnish with fresh strawberries just before serving.

Enjoy this luscious and fruity Strawberry Tiramisu as a delightful dessert that's perfect for warmer seasons or any special occasion!

Raspberry Chocolate Tart

Ingredients:

For the Chocolate Tart Shell:

- 1 1/2 cups all-purpose flour
- 1/4 cup unsweetened cocoa powder
- 1/2 cup confectioners' sugar
- 1/4 teaspoon salt
- 3/4 cup unsalted butter, cold and cut into small pieces
- 1 large egg yolk
- 2 tablespoons ice water

For the Chocolate Ganache Filling:

- 8 ounces dark chocolate, finely chopped
- 1 cup heavy cream
- 2 tablespoons unsalted butter
- 1 teaspoon vanilla extract

For Topping:

- Fresh raspberries
- Confectioners' sugar for dusting

Instructions:

For the Chocolate Tart Shell:

Prepare the Dough:
- In a food processor, combine the flour, cocoa powder, confectioners' sugar, and salt. Pulse to mix.
- Add the cold, cubed butter, and pulse until the mixture resembles coarse crumbs.
- In a small bowl, mix the egg yolk with ice water. Add it to the processor and pulse until the dough just comes together.

Form the Tart Shell:
- Turn the dough out onto a lightly floured surface and gather it into a ball. Flatten into a disk, wrap in plastic wrap, and refrigerate for at least 30 minutes.

Roll Out and Bake:
- Preheat your oven to 375°F (190°C).
- Roll out the chilled dough on a floured surface and fit it into a tart pan. Trim any excess dough.
- Prick the bottom with a fork and line with parchment paper. Fill with pie weights or dried beans.
- Bake for 15 minutes. Remove the weights and parchment paper, then bake for an additional 10 minutes or until the crust is set. Let it cool.

For the Chocolate Ganache Filling:

Prepare Ganache:
- Place the finely chopped dark chocolate in a heatproof bowl.
- In a small saucepan, heat the cream until it just starts to simmer. Pour it over the chocolate.
- Let it sit for a minute, then stir until the chocolate is melted and the ganache is smooth.
- Add the butter and vanilla extract, stirring until smooth and glossy.

Fill the Tart Shell:
- Pour the chocolate ganache into the cooled tart shell. Smooth the top with a spatula.

Chill:
- Refrigerate the tart for at least 2-3 hours or until the chocolate ganache is set.

Top with Raspberries:
- Arrange fresh raspberries on top of the set chocolate ganache.

Dust with Confectioners' Sugar:
- Dust the top of the tart with confectioners' sugar just before serving.

This Raspberry Chocolate Tart is a show-stopping dessert with the perfect balance of rich chocolate and bright, tart raspberries. Enjoy this elegant treat for special occasions or when you're craving a delightful chocolatey indulgence!

Coffee and Walnut Cake

Ingredients:

For the Cake:

- 1 cup unsalted butter, softened
- 1 cup granulated sugar
- 4 large eggs
- 2 cups all-purpose flour
- 2 teaspoons baking powder
- 3 tablespoons instant coffee, dissolved in 3 tablespoons hot water
- 1/2 cup chopped walnuts
- 1 teaspoon vanilla extract

For the Coffee Buttercream:

- 1 cup unsalted butter, softened
- 2 cups confectioners' sugar
- 2 tablespoons instant coffee, dissolved in 2 tablespoons hot water
- Chopped walnuts for decoration (optional)

Instructions:

For the Cake:

Preheat the Oven:
- Preheat your oven to 350°F (180°C). Grease and line two 8-inch round cake pans with parchment paper.

Cream Butter and Sugar:
- In a large bowl, cream together the softened butter and granulated sugar until light and fluffy.

Add Eggs:
- Add the eggs one at a time, beating well after each addition.

Combine Dry Ingredients:
- In a separate bowl, sift together the flour and baking powder.

Add Coffee and Walnuts:

- Dissolve the instant coffee in hot water and add it to the wet ingredients. Mix well.
- Fold in the sifted dry ingredients until just combined.
- Stir in the chopped walnuts and vanilla extract.

Bake:
- Divide the batter evenly between the prepared cake pans.
- Bake in the preheated oven for approximately 25-30 minutes or until a toothpick inserted into the center comes out clean.

Cool:
- Allow the cakes to cool in the pans for a few minutes before transferring them to a wire rack to cool completely.

For the Coffee Buttercream:

Prepare Coffee Buttercream:
- Dissolve instant coffee in hot water and let it cool.
- In a large bowl, beat the softened butter until creamy.
- Gradually add the confectioners' sugar, beating well after each addition.
- Add the dissolved coffee and beat until smooth and fluffy.

Assembling the Cake:

Layer and Frost:
- Once the cakes are completely cool, spread a layer of coffee buttercream on top of one cake layer.
- Place the second cake layer on top and frost the top and sides with the remaining coffee buttercream.

Decorate:
- Optionally, decorate the cake with additional chopped walnuts on top.

Slice and Serve:
- Slice and serve the Coffee and Walnut Cake. Enjoy with a cup of coffee or tea!

This delightful Coffee and Walnut Cake is perfect for afternoon tea or as a special treat for coffee lovers. The combination of moist cake layers and rich coffee buttercream creates a delicious and comforting dessert.

Orange Chocolate Mousse

Ingredients:

- 8 ounces (about 225g) semi-sweet or bittersweet chocolate, finely chopped
- 3 large eggs, separated
- 1/4 cup granulated sugar
- 1 teaspoon vanilla extract
- Zest of 1 orange
- 1/2 cup fresh orange juice
- Pinch of salt
- 1 cup heavy cream
- Additional orange zest and chocolate shavings for garnish (optional)

Instructions:

Melt Chocolate:
- In a heatproof bowl, melt the chopped chocolate over a double boiler or in the microwave. Allow it to cool slightly.

Prepare Egg Yolks Mixture:
- In a separate bowl, whisk together the egg yolks, sugar, vanilla extract, and orange zest until well combined.

Add Melted Chocolate:
- Gradually whisk the melted chocolate into the egg yolk mixture until smooth and well incorporated.

Add Orange Juice:
- Stir in the fresh orange juice, ensuring that the mixture remains smooth.

Whip Egg Whites:
- In another clean, dry bowl, whip the egg whites with a pinch of salt until stiff peaks form.

Fold Egg Whites:
- Gently fold the whipped egg whites into the chocolate mixture in two or three additions until no white streaks remain.

Whip Heavy Cream:
- In a separate bowl, whip the heavy cream until it holds stiff peaks.

Fold in Whipped Cream:
- Fold the whipped cream into the chocolate mixture until smooth and well combined.

Chill:
- Divide the mousse into serving glasses or bowls. Refrigerate for at least 2-3 hours or until set.

Garnish and Serve:
- Before serving, you can garnish the Orange Chocolate Mousse with additional orange zest and chocolate shavings if desired.

Serve Chilled:
- Serve the Orange Chocolate Mousse chilled, and enjoy the delightful combination of chocolate and citrus flavors.

This Orange Chocolate Mousse is a light and indulgent dessert that's perfect for special occasions or whenever you're craving a delightful treat. The citrusy twist adds a refreshing element to the classic chocolate mousse.

S'mores Dip

Ingredients:

- 1 cup chocolate chips (milk chocolate or a mix of milk and semi-sweet)
- 1 cup mini marshmallows
- Graham crackers for dipping

Instructions:

Preheat the Oven:

Preheat your oven to 450°F (230°C).

Layer the Chocolate:

Spread the chocolate chips evenly in the bottom of a heatproof skillet or a shallow baking dish.

Add Marshmallows:

Sprinkle the mini marshmallows over the chocolate, covering it completely.

Bake:

Place the skillet or baking dish in the preheated oven and bake for about 5-7 minutes or until the marshmallows turn golden brown. Keep a close eye on it to prevent burning.

Serve:

Once the marshmallows are golden and gooey, remove the dip from the oven. Be cautious as the dip will be hot.

Dip with Graham Crackers:

Serve the s'mores dip immediately with graham crackers for dipping. The crackers can be used to scoop up the chocolate and marshmallow goodness.

Enjoy:

> Invite everyone to dig in and enjoy the deliciousness reminiscent of traditional s'mores.

Optional Variations:

Drizzle with Caramel or Peanut Butter:

- Add an extra layer of flavor by drizzling caramel or peanut butter over the melted marshmallows before serving.

Top with Crushed Graham Crackers:

- Sprinkle crushed graham crackers on top of the marshmallows for added texture and to enhance the s'mores experience.

Use Different Chocolate:

- Experiment with different types of chocolate chips, such as dark chocolate or white chocolate, to customize the flavor to your liking.

S'mores dip is a fantastic treat for gatherings, parties, or a cozy night in. It's easy to make and offers a fun and interactive dessert experience.

Lemon Poppy Seed Cake

Ingredients:

For the Cake:

- 2 cups all-purpose flour
- 1 tablespoon poppy seeds
- 1 teaspoon baking powder
- 1/2 teaspoon baking soda
- 1/4 teaspoon salt
- 1 cup unsalted butter, softened
- 1 and 1/2 cups granulated sugar
- 4 large eggs
- 1 teaspoon vanilla extract
- Zest of 2 lemons
- 1/4 cup fresh lemon juice
- 1 cup buttermilk

For the Glaze:

- 1 cup powdered sugar
- 2 tablespoons fresh lemon juice
- Zest of 1 lemon

Instructions:

Preheat the Oven:

Preheat your oven to 350°F (175°C). Grease and flour a bundt pan.

Mix Dry Ingredients:

In a bowl, whisk together the flour, poppy seeds, baking powder, baking soda, and salt. Set aside.

Cream Butter and Sugar:

In a large mixing bowl, cream together the softened butter and granulated sugar until light and fluffy.

Add Eggs and Flavorings:

Add the eggs one at a time, beating well after each addition. Mix in the vanilla extract, lemon zest, and lemon juice.

Alternate Dry Ingredients and Buttermilk:

Gradually add the dry ingredients to the wet ingredients, alternating with the buttermilk. Begin and end with the dry ingredients, mixing until just combined.

Bake:

Pour the batter into the prepared bundt pan and smooth the top. Bake in the preheated oven for about 45-50 minutes or until a toothpick inserted into the center comes out clean.

Cool:

Allow the cake to cool in the pan for about 15 minutes, then transfer it to a wire rack to cool completely.

Prepare the Glaze:

In a small bowl, whisk together the powdered sugar, fresh lemon juice, and lemon zest until smooth.

Glaze the Cake:

Once the cake is completely cooled, drizzle the lemon glaze over the top. You can let the glaze set before serving.

Serve:

Slice and serve the lemon poppy seed cake, either as is or with a dollop of whipped cream or a scoop of vanilla ice cream.

This lemon poppy seed cake is perfect for any occasion, offering a burst of citrus flavor and a delightful texture from the poppy seeds. Enjoy it with a cup of tea or coffee for a delightful treat.

Gingerbread Cookies

Ingredients:

For the Cookies:

- 3 cups all-purpose flour
- 1 teaspoon baking soda
- 1/4 teaspoon salt
- 1 tablespoon ground ginger
- 1 tablespoon ground cinnamon
- 1/2 teaspoon ground cloves
- 1/2 teaspoon ground nutmeg
- 3/4 cup unsalted butter, softened
- 3/4 cup brown sugar, packed
- 1/2 cup molasses
- 1 large egg
- 1 teaspoon vanilla extract

For the Royal Icing:

- 2 cups powdered sugar
- 1 large egg white
- 1/2 teaspoon vanilla extract
- Food coloring (optional)

Instructions:

For the Cookies:

Preheat the Oven:

> Preheat your oven to 350°F (175°C) and line baking sheets with parchment paper.

Mix Dry Ingredients:

> In a medium bowl, whisk together the flour, baking soda, salt, ginger, cinnamon, cloves, and nutmeg. Set aside.

Cream Butter and Sugar:

In a large bowl, cream together the softened butter and brown sugar until light and fluffy.

Add Molasses, Egg, and Vanilla:

Beat in the molasses, then add the egg and vanilla extract. Mix until well combined.

Combine Wet and Dry Ingredients:

Gradually add the dry ingredients to the wet ingredients, mixing until a soft dough forms.

Chill the Dough:

Divide the dough into two portions, wrap each in plastic wrap, and refrigerate for at least 1 hour or until the dough is firm.

Roll and Cut Shapes:

On a floured surface, roll out one portion of the dough to about 1/4 inch thickness. Use gingerbread cookie cutters to cut out shapes and transfer them to the prepared baking sheets.

Bake:

Bake in the preheated oven for 8-10 minutes or until the edges are set. Allow the cookies to cool on the baking sheets for a few minutes before transferring them to a wire rack to cool completely.

For the Royal Icing:

Prepare the Icing:

In a bowl, whisk together the powdered sugar, egg white, and vanilla extract until smooth. If the consistency is too thick, add a little water; if too thin, add more powdered sugar.

Color the Icing (Optional):

Divide the icing into smaller bowls and add food coloring if desired.

Decorate the Cookies:

Once the cookies are completely cooled, use a piping bag or a small spatula to decorate them with the royal icing. Allow the icing to set before storing or serving.

These gingerbread cookies are not only delicious but also perfect for festive decoration. Enjoy making and sharing them during the holiday season!